TEA-CUP READING AND FORTUNE-TELLING BY TEA LEAVES

By A Highland Seer

With Ten Illustrations

Vintage Classics

CONTENTS

ILLUSTRATIONS

PREFACE

It is somewhat curious that among the great number of books on occult science and all forms of divination which have been published in the English language there should be none dealing exclusively with the Tea-cup Reading and the Art of Telling Fortunes by the Tea-leaves: notwithstanding that it is one of the most common forms of divination practised by the peasants of Scotland and by village fortune-tellers in all parts of this country. In many of the cheaper handbooks to Fortune-telling by Cards or in other ways only brief references to the Tea-cup method are given; but only too evidently by writers who are merely acquainted with it by hearsay and have not made a study of it for themselves.

This is probably because the Reading of the Tea-cups affords but little opportunity to the Seer of extracting money from credulous folk; a reason why it was never adopted by the gypsy soothsayers, who preferred the more obviously lucrative methods of crossing the palm with gold or silver, or of charging a fee for manipulating a pack of playing-cards.

Reading the Cup is essentially a domestic form of Fortune-telling to be practised at home, and with success by anyone who will take the trouble to master the simple rules laid down in these pages: and it is in the hope that it will provide a basis for much innocent and inexpensive amusement and recreation round the tea-table at home, as well as for a more serious study of an interesting subject, that this little guide-book to the science is confidently offered to the public.

CHAPTER I
INTRODUCTION TO THE ART OF DIVINATION FROM TEA-LEAVES

It seems highly probable that at no previous period of the world's history have there been so many persons as there are at the present moment anxious to ascertain in advance, if that be humanly possible, a knowledge of at least 'what a day may bring forth.' The incidence of the greatest of all wars, which has resulted in sparse news of those from whom they are separated, and produces a state of uncertainty as to what the future holds in store for each of the inhabitants of the British Empire, is, of course, responsible for this increase in a perfectly sane and natural curiosity; with its inevitable result, a desire to employ any form of divination in the hope that some light may haply be cast upon the darkness and obscurity of the future.

It is unfortunately the case, as records of the police-courts have recently shown, that the creation of this demand for foreknowledge of coming events or for information as to the well-being of distant relatives and friends has resulted in the abundant supply of the want by scores of pretended 'Fortune-tellers' and diviners of the Future; who, trading upon the credulity and anxieties of their unfortunate fellow-countrywomen, seek to make a living at their expense.

Now it is an axiom, which centuries of experience have shown to be as sound as those of Euclid himself, that the moment the taint of money enters into the business of reading the Future the accuracy and credit of the Fortune told disappears. The Fortune-teller no longer possesses the singleness of mind or purpose necessary to a clear reading of the symbols he or she consults. The amount of the fee is the first consideration, and this alone is sufficient to obscure the mental vision and to bias the judgment. This applies to the very highest and most conscientious of Fortune-tellers—persons really adept at foreseeing the future when no taint of monetary reward intervenes. The greater number, however, of so-called Fortune-tellers are but charlatans, with the merest smattering of partly-assimilated knowledge of some form of divination or 'character-reading'; whether by the cards, coins, dice, dominoes, hands, crystal, or in any other pretended way. With these, the taint of the money they hope to receive clouds such mind or intuition as they may possess, and it follows that their judgments and prognostications have precisely the same value as the nostrums of the quack medicine-vendor. They are very different from the

Highlander who, coming to the door of his cottage or bothie at dawn, regards steadfastly the signs and omens he notes in the appearance of the sky, the actions of animals, the flight of birds, and so forth, and derives there from a foresight into the coming events of the opening day. They differ also from the 'spae-wife,' who, manipulating the cup from which she has taken her morning draught of tea, looks at the various forms and shapes the leaves and dregs have taken, and deduces thence such simple horary prognostications as the name of the person from whom 'postie' will presently bring up the glen a letter or a parcel or a remittance of money; or as to whether she is likely to go a journey, or to hear news from across the sea, or to obtain a good price for the hose she has knitted or for the chickens or eggs she is sending to the store-keeper. Here the taint of a money-payment is altogether absent; and no Highland 'spae-wife' or seer would dream of taking a fee for looking into the future on behalf of another person.

It follows, therefore, that provided he or she is equipped with the requisite knowledge and some skill and intuition, the persons most fitted to tell correctly their own fortune are themselves; because they cannot pay themselves for their own prognostications, and the absence of a monetary taint consequently leaves the judgment unbiased. Undoubtedly one of the simplest, most inexpensive and, as the experience of nearly three centuries has proved, most reliable forms of divination within its own proper limits, is that of reading fortunes in tea-cups. Although it cannot be of the greatest antiquity, seeing that tea was not introduced into Britain until the middle of the seventeenth century, and for many years thereafter was too rare and costly to be used by the great bulk of the population, the practice of reading the tea-leaves doubtless descends from the somewhat similar form of divination known to the Greeks as "κοταβος" by which fortune in love was discovered by the particular splash made by wine thrown out of a cup into a metal basin. A few spae-wives still practise this method by throwing out the tea-leaves into the saucer, but the reading of the symbols as they are originally formed in the cup is undoubtedly the better method.

Any person after a study of this book and by carefully following the principles here laid down may with practice quickly learn to read the horary fortunes that the tea-leaves foretell. It should be distinctly understood, however, that tea-cup fortunes are only horary, or dealing with the events of the hour or the succeeding twenty-four hours at furthest. The immediately forthcoming events are those which cast their shadows, so to speak, within the circle of the cup. In this way the tea-leaves may be consulted once a day, and many of the minor happenings of life foreseen with considerable accuracy, according to the skill in discerning the symbols and the intuition required to interpret them which may be possessed by the seer. Adepts like the Highland peasant-women can and do foretell events that subsequently occur, and that with remarkable accuracy. Practice and the acquirement of a knowledge of the signification of the various symbols is all that is necessary in order to become proficient and to tell one's fortune and that of one's friends with skill and judgment.

There is, of course, a scientific reason for all forms of divination practised without hope or promise of reward. Each person carries in himself his own Destiny. Events do not happen to people by chance, but are invariably the result of some past cause. For instance, in the last years a man becomes a soldier who had never intended to pursue a military career. This does not happen to him by chance, but because of the prior occurrence of la European war in which his country was engaged. The outbreak of war is similarly the result of other causes, none of which happened by chance, but were founded by still remoter occurrences. It is the same with the Future. That which a person does today as a result of something that happened in the past, will in its turn prove the cause of something that will happen at some future date. The mere act of doing something today sets in motion forces that in process of time will inevitably bring about some entirely unforeseen event.

This event is not decreed by Fate or Providence, but by the person who by the committal of some act unconsciously compels the occurrence of some future event which he does not foresee. In other words, a man decrees his own destiny and shapes his own ends by his actions, whether Providence rough-hew them or not. Now this being so, it follows that he carries his destiny with him, and the more powerful his mind and intellect the more clearly is this seen to be the case. Therefore it is possible for a person's mind, formed as the result of past events over which he had no control, to foresee by an effort what will occur in the future as the result of acts deliberately done. Since it is given to but few, and that not often of intention, to see actually what is about to happen in a vision or by means of what is called the 'second sight,' some machinery must be provided in the form of symbols from which an interpretation of the future can be made. It matters little what the method or nature of the symbols chosen is—dice or dominoes, cards or tea-leaves. What matters is that the person shaking the dice, shuffling the dominoes, cutting the cards or turning the tea-cup, is by these very acts transferring from his mind where they lie hidden even from himself the shadows of coming events which by his own actions in the past he has already predetermined shall occur in the future. It only remains for someone to read and interpret these symbols correctly in order to ascertain something of what is likely to happen; and it is here that singleness of purpose and freedom from ulterior motives are necessary in order to avoid error and to form a true and clear judgment.

This is the serious and scientific explanation of the little-understood and less-comprehended action of various forms of divination having for their object the throwing of a little light upon the occult. Of all these forms perhaps divination by tea-leaves is the simplest, truest, and most easily learned. Even if the student is disinclined to attach much importance to what he sees in the cup, the reading of the tea-leaves forms a sufficiently innocent and amusing recreation for the breakfast- or tea-table; and the man who finds a lucky sign such as an anchor or a tree in his cup, or the maiden who discovers a pair of heart-shaped groups of leaves in conjunction with a ring, will be suffering no harm in thus deriving encouragement for the future, even should they attach no importance to their occurrence, but merely treat them as an occasion for harmless mirth and badinage.

Whether, however, the tea-leaves be consulted seriously or in mere sport and love of amusement, the methods set forth in succeeding chapters should be carefully followed, and the significations of the pictures and symbols formed in the cup scrupulously accepted as correct, for reasons which are explained in a subsequent chapter.

CHAPTER II
RITUAL AND METHOD OF USING THE TEA-CUP

The best kind of tea to use if tea-cup reading is to be followed is undoubtedly China tea, the original tea imported into this country and still the best for all purposes. Indian tea and the cheaper mixtures contain so much dust and so many fragments of twigs and stems as often to be quite useless for the purposes of divination, as they will not combine to form pictures, or symbols clearly to be discerned.

The best shape of cup to employ is one with a wide opening at the top and a bottom not too small. Cups with almost perpendicular sides are very difficult to read, as the symbols cannot be seen properly, and the same may be said of small cups. A plain-surfaced breakfast-cup is perhaps the best to use; and the interior should be white and have no pattern printed upon it, as this confuses the clearness of the picture presented by the leaves, as does any fluting or eccentricity of shape.

The ritual to be observed is very simple. The tea-drinker should drink the contents of his or her cup so as to leave only about half a teaspoonful of the beverage remaining. He should next take the cup by the handle in his left hand, rim upwards, and turn it three times from left to right in one fairly rapid swinging movement. He should then very slowly and carefully invert it over the saucer and leave it there for a minute, so as to permit of all moisture draining away.

If he approaches the oracle at all seriously he should during the whole of these proceedings concentrate his mind upon his future Destiny, and 'will' that the symbols forming under the guidance of his hand and arm (which in their turn are, of course, directed by his brain) shall correctly represent what is destined to happen to him in the future.

If, however, he or she is not in such deadly earnest, but merely indulging in a harmless pastime, such an effort of concentration need not be made. The 'willing' is, of course, akin to 'wishing' when cutting the cards in another time-honoured form of fortune-telling.

The cup to be read should be held in the hand and turned about in order to read the symbols without disturbing them, which will not happen if the moisture has been properly drained away. The handle of the cup represents the consultant and is akin to the 'house' in divination by the cards. By this fixed point judgment is made as to events approaching the 'house' of the consultant, journeys away from home, messages or visitors to be expected, relative distance, and so forth. The advantage of employing a cup instead of a saucer is here apparent.

'The bottom of the cup represents the remoter future foretold; the side events not so far distant; and matters symbolised near the rim those that may be expected to occur quickly. The nearer the symbols approach the handle in all three cases the nearer to fulfilment will be the events prognosticated.

If this simple ritual has been correctly carried out the tea-leaves, whether many or few, will be found distributed about the bottom and sides of the cup. The fortune may be equally well told whether there are many leaves or few; but of course there must be some, and therefore the tea should not have been made in a pot provided with one of the patent arrangements that stop the leaves from issuing from the spout when the beverage is poured into the cups. There is nothing to beat one of the plain old-fashioned earthenware teapots, whether for the purpose of preparing a palatable beverage or for that of providing the means of telling a fortune.

CHAPTER III
GENERAL PRINCIPLES TO BE OBSERVED IN READING THE CUP

The interior of the tea-cup when it is ready to be consulted will exhibit the leaves scattered apparently in a fortuitous and accidental manner, but really in accordance with the muscular action of the left arm as controlled by the mind at whose bidding it has worked. These scattered leaves will form lines and circles of dots or small leaves and dust combined with stems, and groups of leaves in larger or smaller patches: apparently in meaningless confusion.

Careful notice should now be taken of all the shapes and figures formed inside the cup. These should be viewed front different positions, so that their meaning becomes clear. It is not very easy at first to see what the shapes really are, but after looking at them carefully they become plainer. The different shapes and figures in the cup must be taken together in a general reading. Bad indications will be balanced by good ones; some good ones will be strengthened by others, and so on.

It is now the business of the seer—whether the consultant or some adept to whom he has handed the cup to be read—to find some fairly close resemblance between the groups formed by the leaves and various natural or artificial objects. This part of the performance resembles the looking for 'pictures in the fire' as practised by children in nurseries and school-rooms and occasionally by people of a larger growth. Actual representations of such things as trees, animals, birds, anchors, crowns, coffins, flowers, and so forth may by the exercise of the powers of observation and imagination be discerned, as well as squares, triangles, and crosses. Each of these possesses, as a symbol, some fortunate or unfortunate signification. Such signs may be either large or small, and their relative importance must be judged according to their size. Supposing the symbol observed should be that indicating the receipt of a legacy, for instance: if small it would mean that the inheritance would be but trifling, if large that it would be substantial, while if leaves grouped to form a resemblance to a coronet accompany the sign for a legacy, a title would probably descend upon the consultant at the same time. The meaning of all the symbols of this nature likely to be formed by the fortuitous arrangement of leaves in a tea-cup is fully set forth in the concluding chapter; and it is unnecessary therefore to enlarge upon this branch of the subject.

There are, however, several points of a more general character that must be considered before it is possible to form an accurate judgment of the fortune displayed. For instance, isolated leaves or groups of a few leaves or stems frequently form letters of the alphabet or numbers. These letters and numbers possess meanings which must be sought in conjunction with other signs. If near a letter L is seen a small square or oblong leaf, or if a number of very small dots form such a square or oblong, it indicates that a letter or parcel will be received from somebody whose surname (not Christian name) begins with an L. If the combined symbol appears near the handle and near the rim of the cup, the letter is close at hand; if in the bottom there will be delay in its receipt. If the sign of a letter is accompanied by the appearance of a bird flying towards the 'house' it means a telegraphic despatch: if flying away from the house the consultant will have to send the telegram. Birds flying always indicate news of some sort.

Again, the dust in the tea and the smaller leaves and stems frequently form lines of dots. These are significant of a journey, and their extent and direction shows its length and the point of the compass towards which it will extend: the handle for this purpose being considered as due south. If the consultant is at home and lines lead from the handle right round the cup and back to the handle, it shows that he will return; if they end before getting back to the handle, and especially if a resemblance to a house appears where the journey line ends, it betokens removal to some other place. If the consultant be away from home, lines leading to the handle show a return home, and if free from crosses or other symbols of delay that the return will be speedy: otherwise it will be postponed. The occurrence of a numeral may indicate the number of days, or if in connection with a number of small dots grouped around the sign of a letter, a present or a legacy, the amount of the remittance in the former, the number of presents to be expected, or the amount of the legacy coming. Dots surrounding a symbol always indicate money coming in some form or other, according to the nature of the symbol.

It will be seen that to read a fortune in the tea-cup with any real approach to accuracy and a serious attempt to derive a genuine forecast from the cup the seer must not be in a hurry. He or she must not only study the general appearance of the horoscope displayed before him, and decide upon the resemblance of the groups of leaves to natural or artificial objects, each of which possesses a separate significance, but must also balance the bad and good, the lucky and unlucky symbols, and strike an average. For instance, a large bouquet of flowers, which is a fortunate sign, would outweigh in importance one or two minute crosses, which in this case would merely signify some small delay in the realisation of success; whereas one large cross in a prominent position would be a warning of disaster that would be little, if at all, mitigated by the presence of small isolated flowers, however lucky individually these may be. This is on the same principle as that by which astrologers judge a horoscope, when, after computing the aspects of the planets towards each other, the Sun and Moon, the Ascendant, Mid-heaven, and the significator of the Native, they balance the good aspects against the bad, the strong against the weak, the Benefics against the Malefics, and so strike an average. In a similar way the lucky and unlucky, signs in a tea-cup must be balanced one against the other and an average struck: and in this connection it may be pointed out that symbols which stand out clearly and distinctly by themselves are of more importance than those with difficulty to be discerned amid cloudlike masses of shapeless leaves. When these clouds obscure or surround a lucky sign they weaken its force, and vice versa. In tea-cup reading, however, the fortune told must be regarded chiefly as of a horary character, not, as with an astrological horoscope, that of a whole life; and where it is merely indulged in as a light amusement to while away a few minutes after a meal such nicety of judgment is not called for. The seer will just glance at the cup, note the sign for a letter from someone, or that for a journey to the seaside or the proximity of a gift, or an offer of marriage, and pass on to another cup.

It should be observed that some cups when examined will present no features of interest, or will be so clouded and muddled that no clear meaning is to be read in them. In such a case the seer should waste no time over them. Either the consultant has not concentrated his or her attention upon the business in hand when turning the cup, or his destiny is so obscured by the indecision of his mind or the vagueness of his ideas that it is unable to manifest itself by symbols. Persons who consult the tea-leaves too frequently often find this muddled state of things to supervene. Probably once a week will be often enough to look into the future, although there is something to be said for the Highland custom of examining the leaves of the morning cup of tea in order to obtain some insight into the events the day may be expected to bring forth. To 'look in the cup' three or four times a day, as some silly folk do, is simply to ask for contradictory manifestations and consequent bewilderment, and is symptomatic of the idle, empty, bemused minds that prompt to such ill-advised conduct.

Of course the tea-cup may be employed solely for the purpose of asking what is known to astrologers as 'a horary question', such, for instance, as 'Shall I hear from my lover in France, and when?' In this case the attention of the consultant when turning the cup must be concentrated solely on this single point, and the seer will regard the shapes taken by the tea-leaves solely in this connection in order to give a definite and satisfactory answer. An example of this class of horary question is included among the illustrations (Fig. 10).

CHAPTER IV
AN ALPHABETICAL LIST OF SYMBOLS WITH THEIR SIGNIFICATIONS

A question that will very naturally occur to persons of an enquiring turn of mind in regard to the figures and symbols seen in the tea-cup is: Why should one symbol necessarily signify one thing and not something quite different?

The answer, of course, is that the meanings given to the symbols are purely arbitrary, and that there is no scientific reason why one should signify one thing and not another. There is no real reason why the ace of clubs, for instance, should not be considered the 'House Card' instead of the nine of hearts, or why the double four in dominoes should signify an invitation instead of a wedding, like the double three.

It is obviously necessary, however, in attempting to read the future by means of any kind of symbols, whether pips, dots, numbers or anything else, to fix beforehand upon some definite meaning to be attributed to each separate symbol and to hold fast to this meaning in all events. In the case of tea-leaves, where the symbols are not mere 'conventional signs' or numbers but actual figures like the pictures seen in the fire or those envisaged in dreams, there is no doubt that the signification of most of them is the result of empyrical experience. Generations of spae-wives have found that the recurrence of a certain figure in the cup has corresponded with the occurrence of a certain event in the future lives of the various persons who have consulted them: and this empyrical knowledge has been handed down from seer to seer until a sufficient deposit of tradition has been formed from which it has been found possible to compile a detailed list of the most important symbols and to attach to each a traditional meaning. These significations have been collected by the writer—in a desultory manner—over a long period of years chiefly from spae-wives in both Highland and Lowland Scotland, but also in Cornwall, on Dartmoor, in Middle England, in Gloucestershire and

Northumberland. Occasionally it has been found that a different meaning is attributed to a symbol by one seer from that given it by another. In such cases an alternative signification might, of course, have been given here, but as the essence of all such significations is that they shall be stable and unvarying, the writer has fixed upon whichever meaning has been most widely attributed to the symbol or appears to have the best authority for its adoption, so that the element of doubt may be excluded.

Although included in their alphabetical order in the list which follows, there are certain figures and symbols which are of so common occurrence and bear such definite interpretation that it is advisable to refer to them here in detail. Certain symbols are invariably signs of approaching good-fortune: certain others of threatened ill-luck. Among the former may be mentioned triangles, stars, trefoil or clover-leaves, anchors, trees, garlands and flowers, bridges or arches, and crowns. Among the latter, coffins, clouds, crosses, serpents, rats and mice and some wild beasts, hour-glasses, umbrellas, church-steeples, swords and guns, ravens, owls, and monkeys are all ominous symbols.

SYMBOLS AND SIGNIFICATIONS

ABBEY, future ease and freedom from worry.

ACORN, improvement in health, continued health, strength, and good fortune.

AIRCRAFT, unsuccessful projects.

ANCHOR, a lucky sign; success in business and constancy in love; if cloudy, the reverse must be read.

ANGEL, good news, especially good fortune in love.

APES, secret enemies.

APPLES, long life; gain by commerce.

APPLE-TREE, change for the better.

ARCH, a journey abroad.

ARROW, a disagreeable letter from the direction in which it comes.

ASS, misfortune overcome by patience; or a legacy.

AXE, difficulties overcome.

BADGER, long life and prosperity as a bachelor.

BASKET, an addition to the family.

BAT, fruitless journeys or tasks.

BEAR, a long period of travel.

BEASTS, other than those mentioned, foretell misfortune.

BIRDS, a lucky sign; good news if flying, if at rest a fortunate journey.

BOAT, a friend will visit the consultant.

BOUQUET, one of the luckiest of symbols; staunch friends, success, a happy marriage.

BRIDGE, a favourable journey.

BUILDING, a removal.

BULL, slander by some enemy.

BUSH, an invitation into society.

BUTTERFLY, success and pleasure.

CAMEL, a burden to be patiently borne.

CANNON, good fortune.

CAR (MOTOR), and CARRIAGE, approaching wealth, visits from friends.

CART, fluctuations of fortune.

CASTLE, unexpected fortune or a legacy.

CAT, difficulties caused by treachery.

CATHEDRAL, great prosperity.

CATTLE, prosperity.

CHAIN, an early marriage; if broken, trouble in store.

CHAIR, an addition to the family.

CHURCH, a legacy.

CIRCLES, money or presents. They mean that the person whose fortune is read may expect money or presents.

CLOUDS, serious trouble; if surrounded by dots, financial success.

CLOVER, a very lucky sign; happiness and prosperity. At the top of the cup, it will come quickly. As it nears the bottom, it will mean more or less distant.

COCK, much prosperity.

COFFIN, long sickness or sign of death of a near relation or great friend.

COMET, misfortune and trouble.

COMPASSES, a sign of travelling as a profession.

COW, a prosperous sign.

CROSS, a sign of trouble and delay or even death.

CROWN, success and honour.

CROWN AND CROSS, signifies good fortune resulting from death.

DAGGER, favours from friends.

DEER, quarrels, disputes; failure in trade.

DOG, a favourable sign; faithful friends, if at top of cup; in middle of cup, they are untrustworthy; at the bottom means secret enemies.

DONKEY, a legacy long awaited.

DOVE, a lucky symbol; progress in prosperity and affection.

DRAGON, great and sudden changes.

DUCK, increase of wealth by trade.

EAGLE, honour and riches through change of residence.

ELEPHANT, a lucky sign; good health.

FALCON, a persistent enemy.

FERRET, active enemies.

FISH, good news from abroad; if surrounded by dots, emigration.

FLAG, danger from wounds inflicted by an enemy.

FLEUR-DE-LYS, same as LILY (q.v.).

FLOWERS, good fortune, success; a happy marriage.

FOX, treachery by a trusted friend.

FROG, success in love and commerce.

GALLOWS, a sign of good luck.

GOAT, a sign of enemies, and of misfortune to a sailor.

GOOSE, happiness; a successful venture.

GRASSHOPPER, a great friend will become a soldier.

GREYHOUND, a good fortune by strenuous exertion.

GUN, a sign of discord and slander.

HAMMER, triumph over adversity.

HAND, to be read in conjunction with neighbouring symbols and according to what it points.

HARE, a sign of a long journey, or the return of an absent friend. Also of a speedy and fortunate marriage to those who are single.

HARP, marriage, success in love.

HAT, success in life.

HAWK, an enemy.

HEART, pleasures to come; if surrounded by dots, through money; if accompanied by a ring, through marriage.

HEAVENLY BODIES, SUN, MOON AND STARS, signifies happiness and success.

HEN, increase of riches or an addition to the family.

HORSE, desires fulfilled through a prosperous journey.

HORSE-SHOE, a lucky journey or success in marriage and choosing a partner.

HOUR-GLASS, imminent peril.

HOUSE, success in business.

HUMAN FIGURES must be judged according to what they appear to be doing. They are generally good and denote love and marriage.

INTERROGATION (mark of), doubt or disappointment.

IVY, honour and happiness through faithful friends.

JACKAL, a sly animal who need not be feared. A mischief maker of no account.

JOCKEY, successful speculation.

JUG, good health.

KANGAROO, a rival in business or love.

KETTLE, death.

KEY, money, increasing trade, and a good husband or wife.

KITE, a sign of lengthy voyaging and travel leading to honour and dignity.

KNIFE, a warning of disaster through quarrels and enmity.

LADDER, a sign of travel.

LEOPARD, a sign of emigration with subsequent success.

LETTERS, shown by square or oblong tea-leaves, signifies news. Initials near will show surnames of writers; if accompanied by dots they will contain money; if unclouded, good; but if fixed about by clouds, bad news or loss of money.

LILY, at top of cup, health and happiness; a virtuous wife; at bottom, anger and strife.

LINES indicate journeys and their direction, read in conjunction with other signs of travel; wavy lines denote troublesome journeys or losses therein.

LION, greatness through powerful friends.

LYNX, danger of divorce or break off of an engagement.

MAN, a visitor arriving. If the arm is held out, he brings a present. If figure is very clear, he is dark; if indistinct, he is of light complexion.

MERMAID, misfortune, especially to seafaring persons.

MITRE, a sign of honour to a clergyman or through religious agency.

MONKEY, the consultant will be deceived in love.

MOON (as a crescent), prosperity and fortune.

MOUNTAIN, powerful friends; many mountains, equally powerful enemies.

MOUSE, danger of poverty through theft or swindling.

MUSHROOM, sudden separation of lovers after a quarrel.

NOSEGAY, the same as BOUQUET (q.v.).

NUMBERS depends on symbols in conjunction with them.

OAK, very lucky; long life, good health, profitable business, and a happy marriage.

OBLONG FIGURES, family or business squabbles.

OWL, an evil omen, indicative of sickness, poverty, disgrace, a warning against commencing any new enterprise. If the consultant be in love he or she will be deceived.

PALM-TREE, good luck; success in any undertaking. A sign of children to a wife and of a speedy marriage to a maid.

PARROT, a sign of emigration for a lengthy period.

PEACOCK, denotes success and the acquisition of property; also a happy marriage.

PEAR, great wealth and improved social position; success in business, and to a woman a wealthy husband.

PEDESTRIAN, good news; an important appointment.

PHEASANT, a legacy.

PIG, good and bad luck mixed: a faithful lover but envious friends.

PIGEONS, important news if flying; if at rest, domestic bliss and wealth acquired in trade.

PINE-TREE, continuous happiness.

PISTOL, disaster.

RABBIT, fair success in a city or large town.

RAT, treacherous servants; losses through enemies.

RAVEN, death for the aged; disappointment in love, divorce, failure in business, and trouble generally.

RAZOR, lovers' quarrels and separation.

REPTILE, quarrels.

RIDER, good news from overseas regarding financial prospects.

RIFLE, a sign of discord and strife.

RING, a ring means marriage; and if a letter can be found near it, this is the initial of the future spouse. If clouds are near the ring, an unhappy marriage; if all is clear about it, the contrary. A ring right at the bottom means the wedding will not take place.

ROSE, a lucky sign betokening good fortune and happiness.

SAW, trouble brought about by strangers.

SCALES, a lawsuit.

SCEPTRE, a sign of honour from royalty.

SCISSORS, quarrels; illness; separation of lovers.

SERPENT, spiteful enemies; bad luck; illness.

SHARK, danger of death.

SHEEP, success, prosperity.

SHIP, a successful journey.

SNAKES are a sign of bad omen. Great caution is needed to

ward off misfortune.

SPIDER, a sign of money coming to the consultant.

SQUARES, comfort and peace.

STAR, a lucky sign; if surrounded by dots foretells great wealth and honours.

STEEPLE, bad luck.

STRAIGHT LINE, a journey, very pleasant.

STRAIGHT LINES are an indication of peace, happiness, and long life.

SWALLOW, a journey with a pleasant ending.

SWAN, good luck and a happy marriage.

SWORD, dispute, quarrels between lovers; a broken sword, victory of an enemy.

TIMBER, logs of timber indicate business success.

TOAD, deceit and unexpected enemies.

TREES, a lucky sign; a sure indication of prosperity and happiness; surrounded by dots, a fortune in the country.

TRIANGLES, always a sign of good luck and unexpected legacies.

TRIDENT, success and honours in the Navy.

TWISTED FIGURES, disturbances and vexation; grievances if there are many such figures.

UMBRELLA, annoyance and trouble.

UNICORN, scandal.

VULTURE, bitter foes.

WAGON, a sign of approaching poverty.

WAVY LINES, if long and waved, denote losses and vexations. The importance of the lines depends upon the number of them and if heavy or light.

WHEEL, an inheritance about to fall in.

WINDMILL, success in a venturous enterprise.

WOLF, beware of jealous intrigues.

WOMAN, pleasure and happiness; if accompanied by dots, wealth or children. Several women indicate scandal.

WOOD, a speedy marriage.

WORMS indicate secret foes.

YACHT, pleasure and happiness.

YEW-TREE indicates the death of an aged person who will leave his possessions to the consultant.

ZEBRA, travel and adventure in foreign lands.

CHAPTER V

A COLLECTION OF SPECIMEN CUPS, WITH INTERPRETATIONS

The succeeding ten figures are copied from actual tea-cups that have been at different times subjected to the proper ritual by various consultants and duly interpreted by seers. They are selected out of a larger number as being representative of many different classes of horoscope, and they should afford students practical instruction in what symbols to look for, and how to discern them clearly as they turn the cup about and about in their hands.

By reference to the interpretations provided upon the pages facing the illustrations he will be able to ascertain the principles upon which to form a judgment of the cup generally; and this, once he has mastered the method, he will be able to supplement, by consulting the alphabetical list of symbols and their significations in the previous chapter, and in this way will speedily attain proficiency in reading any tea-cup presented for his consideration.

INTERPRETATIONS AND ILLUSTRATIONS

INTERPRETATION
FIG.1

This is a fortunate horoscope. If cup has been turned by a man it shows that he will gain success, honour, and wealth in the profession of a naval officer. If by a woman then her luck is bound up with that of a sailor or marine.

The pistols on the sides show the profession of arms, and the naval gun in the bottom of the cup accompanied by a trident the branch to which he belongs. The on one side and the tree on the other are two of the best signs of promotion, rewards, and prosperity. The house near the pistol pointing towards the handle of the cup indicates the acquisition of property, but as neither tree nor house are surrounded by dots this will be a town, not a country, residence. The repetition of the initial 'L' may show the name of the admiral, ship, or battle in which the officer will win renown. The triangles confirm the other signs of good fortune.

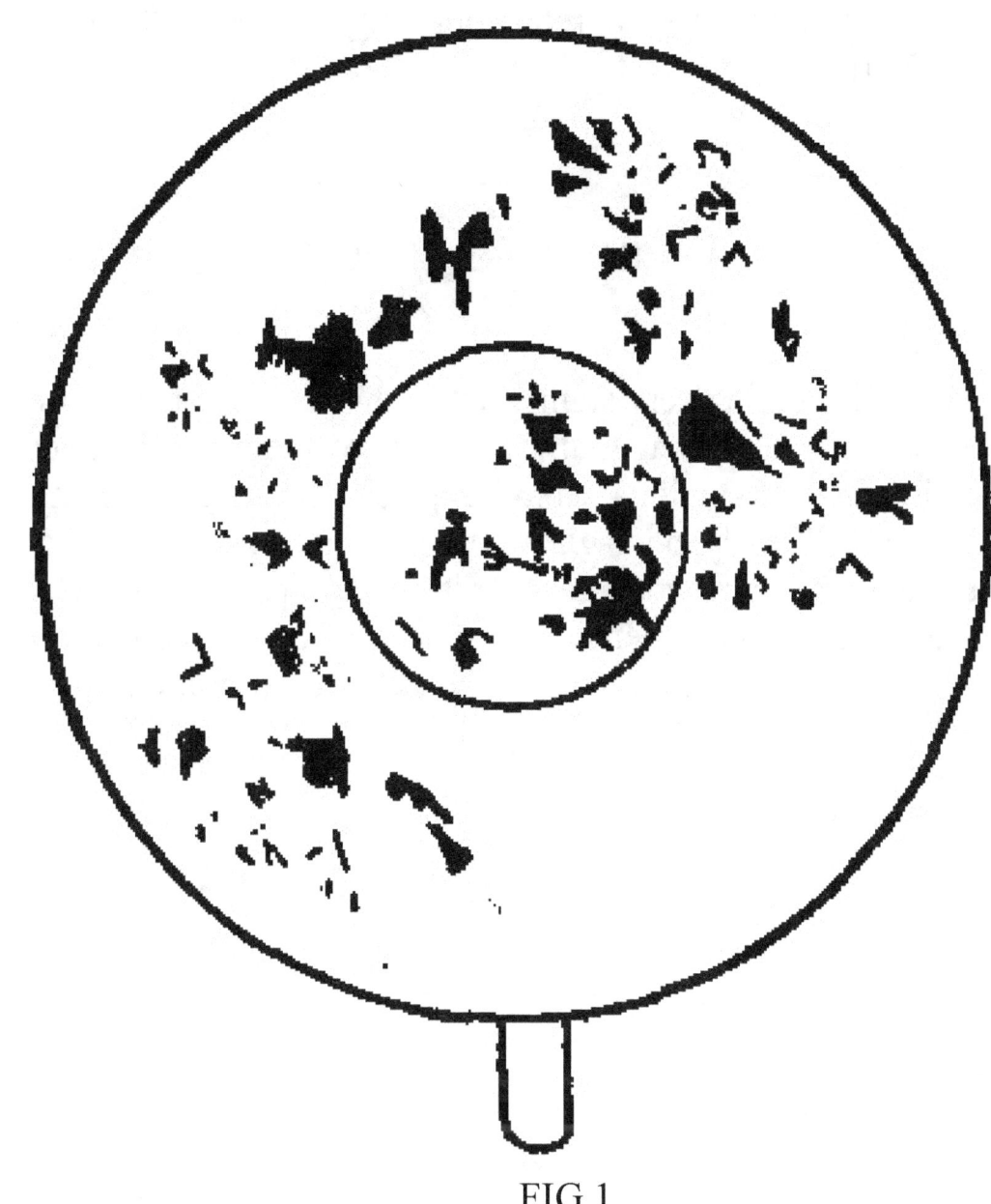

FIG.1

Principal Symbols:—

Two pistols on sides.
A cannon in conjunction with a trident in centre.
A pear.
A tree.
on sides.
A house.
A pair of compasses near the rim.

Several small triangles scattered about. Initial letters 'L' (twice), 'N,' and 'V' (twice).

INTERPRETATION
FIG. 2

There is nothing very significant in this tea-cup. The wavy lines denote a troublesome journey leading to some small amount of luck in connection with a person or place whose name begins with the initial 'E.' The hour-glass near the rim and the place from which the journey starts denotes that it will be undertaken in order to avoid some imminent peril. The numeral '4' conjoined with the sign of a parcel shows that one may be expected in that number of days.

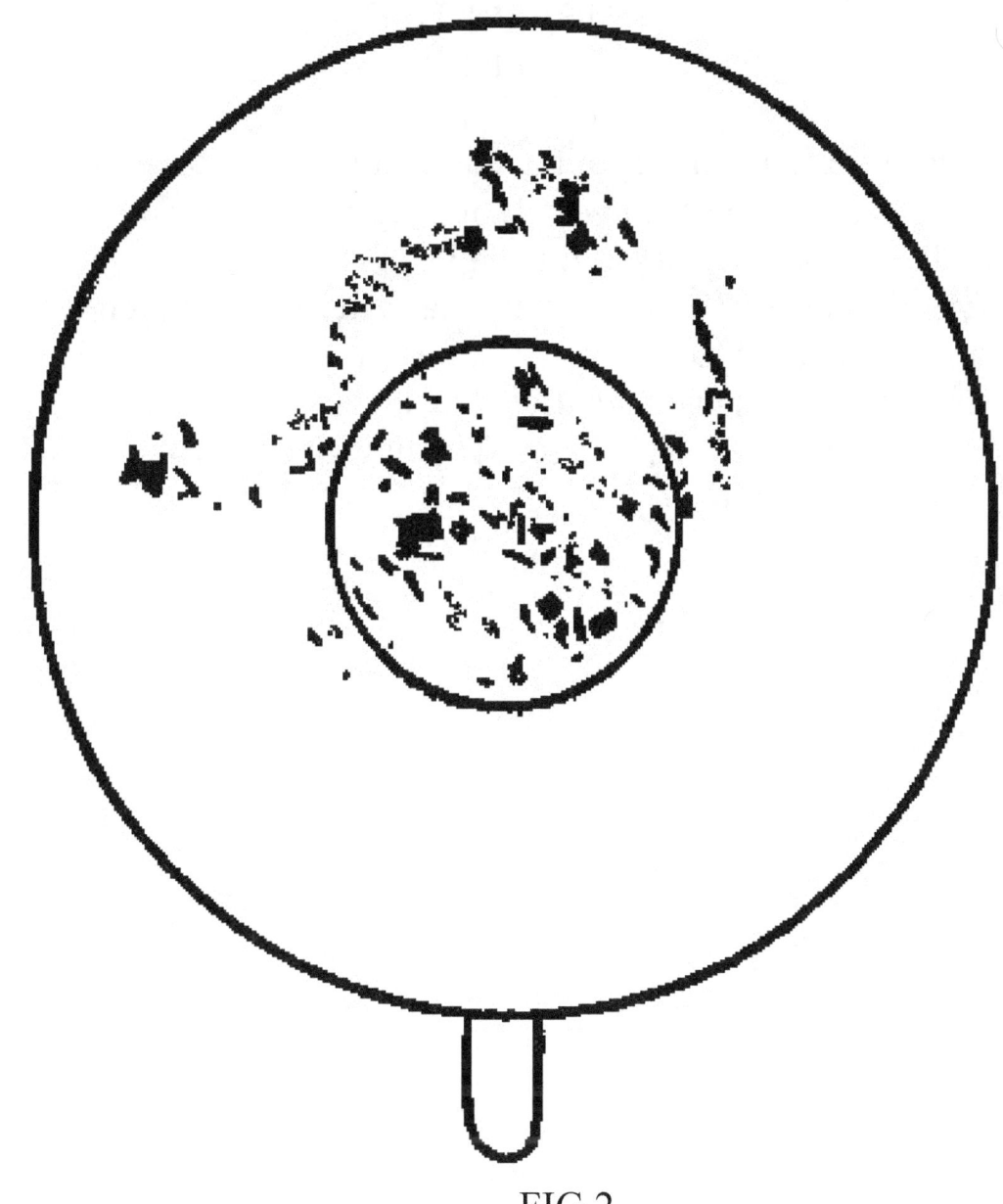

FIG.2

Principal Symbols:—

Wavy lines.
Initial 'E' in conjunction with Horse-shoe.
Hour-glass near rim.
Parcel in conjunction with numeral '4.'

INTERPRETATION
FIG. 3

This shows, by means of the crescent moon on the side, prosperity and fortune as the result of a journey denoted by the lines. The number of triangles in conjunction with the initial 'H' indicates the name commences with that letter, and, being near the rim, at no great distance of time. The bird flying towards and near the handle, accompanied by a triangle and a long envelope, denotes good news from an official source. The flag gives warning of some danger from an enemy.

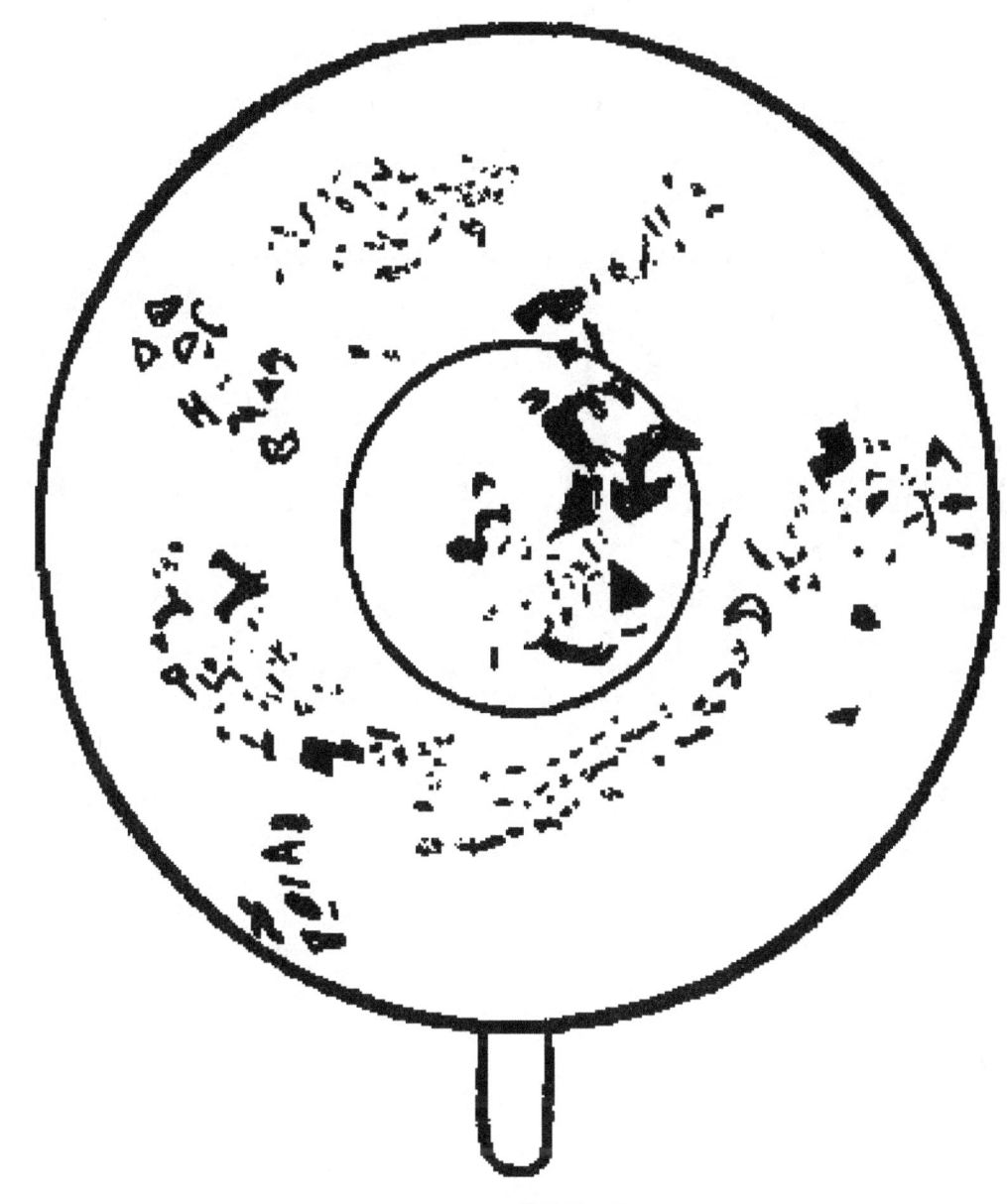

FIG. 3
Principal Symbols:—

Crescent moon.
Bird flying.
Triangles.
Flag.
Initial 'A' in conjunction with sign of letter in official envelope.
Other initials, 'H' and two 'L's.'

INTERPRETATION
FIG. 4

The consultant is about to journey eastward to some large building or institution, shown by the figure at the end of the straight line of dots. There is some confusion in his or her affairs caused by too much indulgence in pleasure and gaiety, denoted by the butterfly involved in obscure groups of tea-leaves near the handle. The tree and the fleur-de-lys (or lily) in the bottom of the cup are, however, signs of eventual success, probably through the assistance of some person whose name begins with an 'N.'

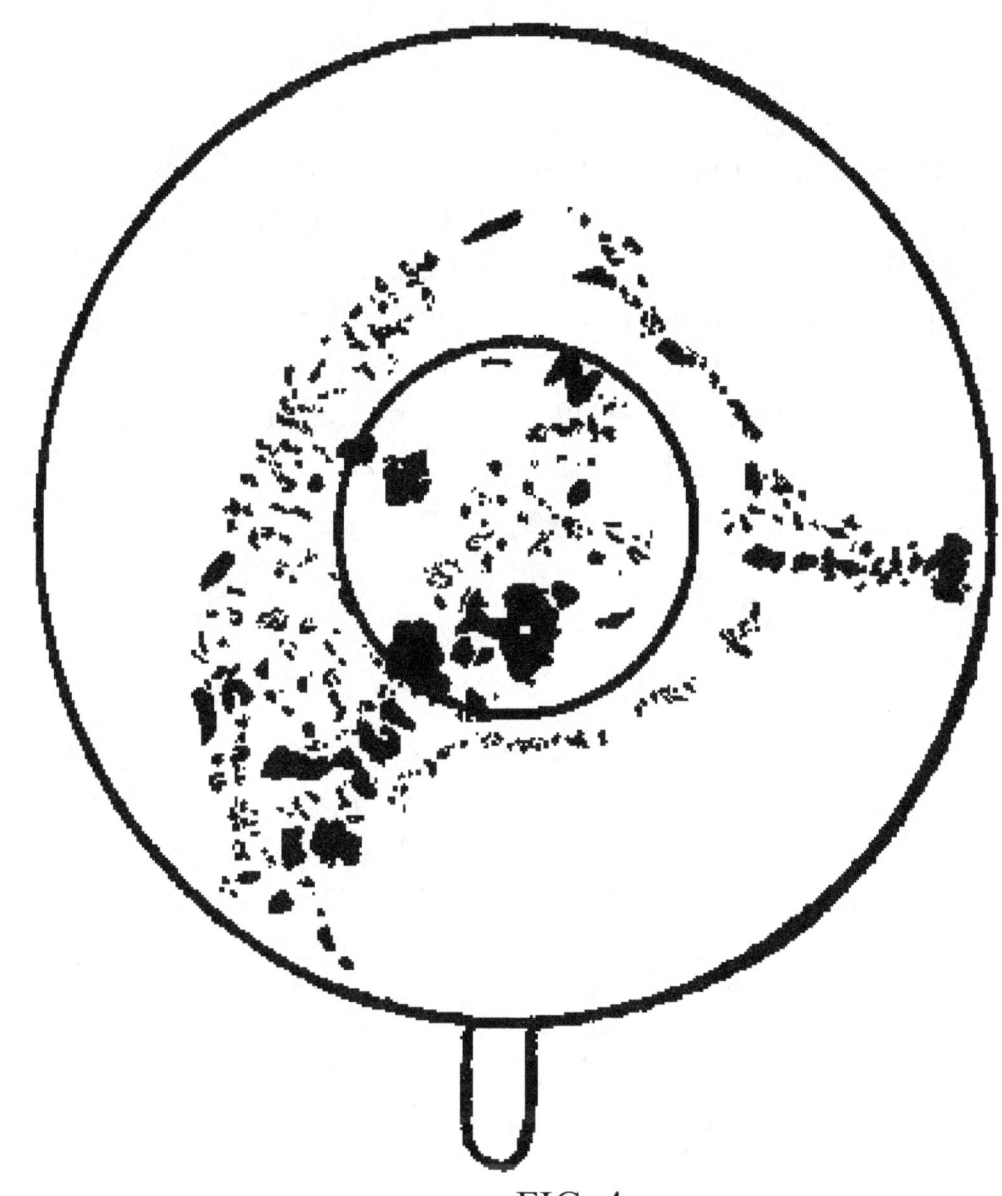

FIG. 4

Principal Symbols:—

Large tree in bottom of cup.
Fleur-de-lys (or lily).
Butterfly on side approaching handle.
Line of dots leading east to Building.
Initials 'N' and 'C.'

INTERPRETATION
FIG.5

A letter is approaching the consultant containing a considerable sum of money, as it is surrounded by dots. The future, shown by the bottom of the cup, is not clear, and betokens adversities; but the presence of the hammer there denotes triumph over these, a sign confirmed by the hat on the side. The consultant will be annoyed by somebody whose name begins with 'J,' and assisted by one bearing the initial 'Y.'

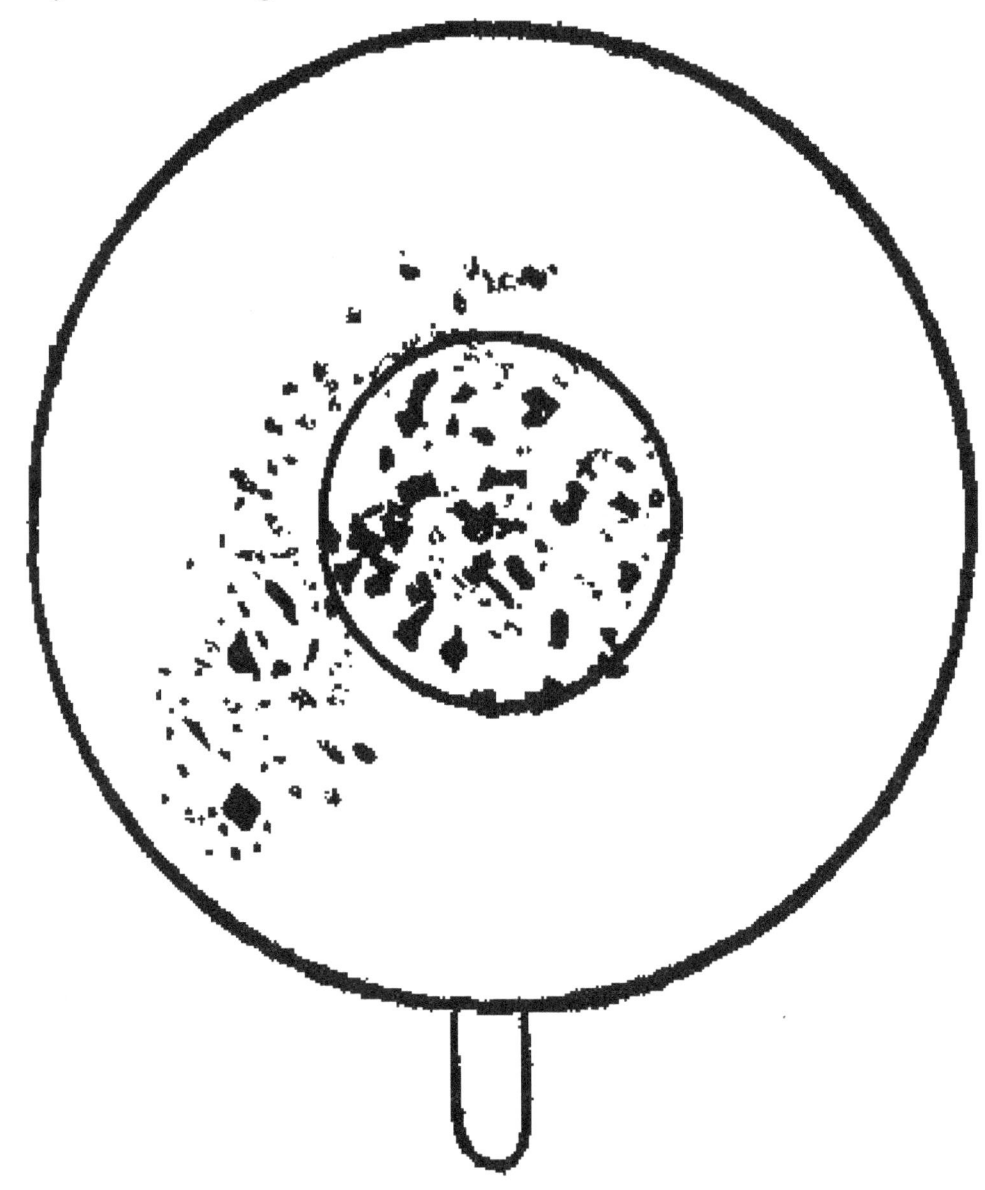

FIG. 5
Principal Symbols:—

Hammer in centre of bottom.
A letter approaching the house, accompanied by
Dots,
Hat,
Initials 'Y' and 'J' (accompanied by small cross).

INTERPRETATION
FIG. 6

A letter containing good news, shown by bird flying and the triangle, may be expected immediately. If from a lover it shows that he is constant and prosperous, owing to the anchor on the side. The large tree on the side indicates happiness and prosperity. A letter will be received from someone whose initial is 'L.' In the bottom of the cup there are signs of minor vexations or delays in connection with someone whose name begins with 'C.'

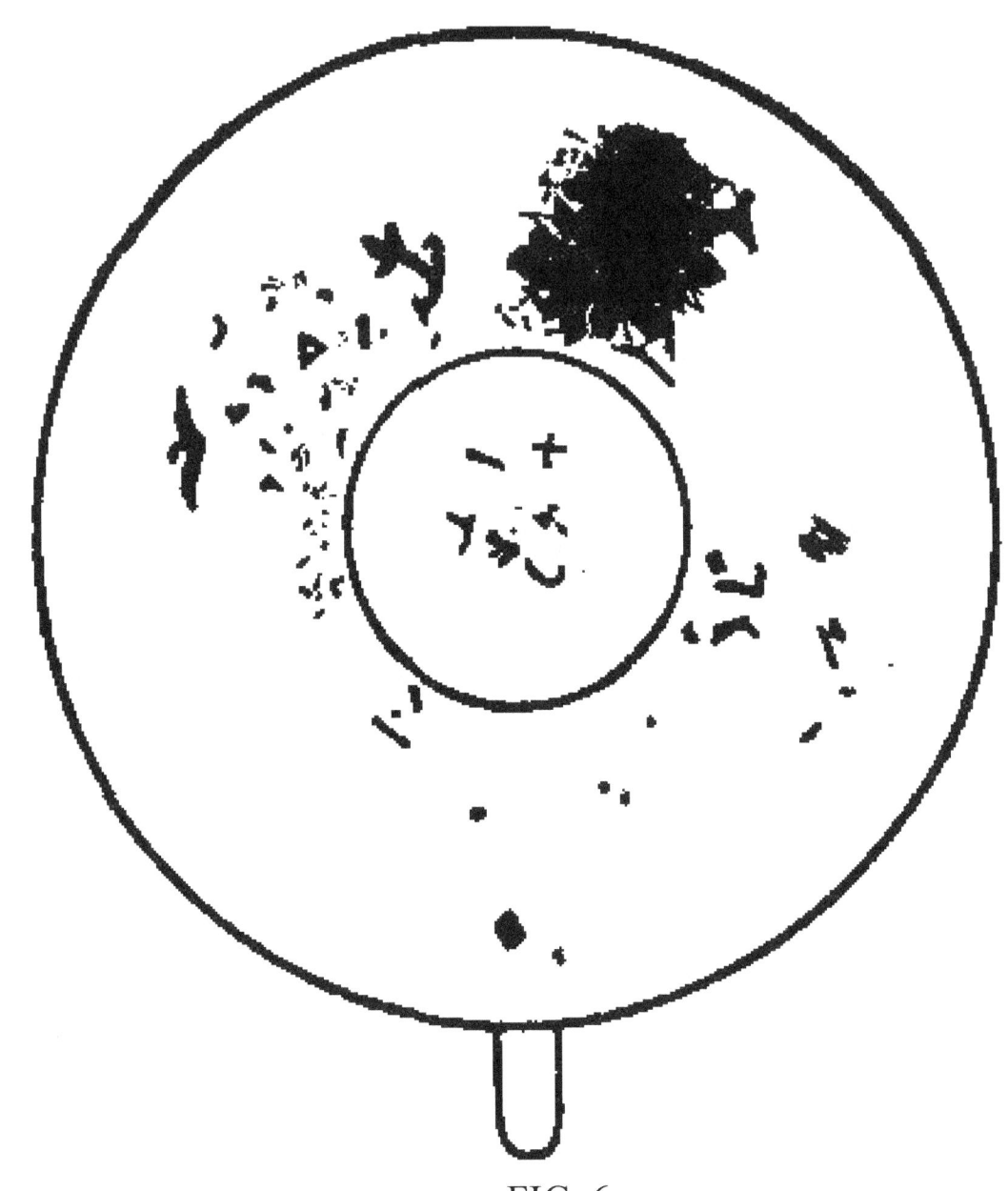

FIG. 6

Principal Symbols:—

Large tree on side.
Anchor on side.
Bird flying high towards handle.
Small cross in bottom.
Letter sign close to handle.
Triangle.
Initial 'L' with letter sign.

Other initials, 'C' and 'H.'

INTERPRETATION
FIG. 7

The two horse-shoes indicate a lucky journey to some large residence in a north-easterly direction, the tree surmounting which denotes that happiness and fortune will be found there and that (as it is surrounded by dots) it is situated in the country. The sitting hen in the bottom of the cup, surmounted by a triangle (to see which properly the illustration must be turned round) is indicative of increased wealth by an unexpected legacy. A letter from someone whose name begins with 'T' will contain a remittance of money, but it may not arrive for some little time.

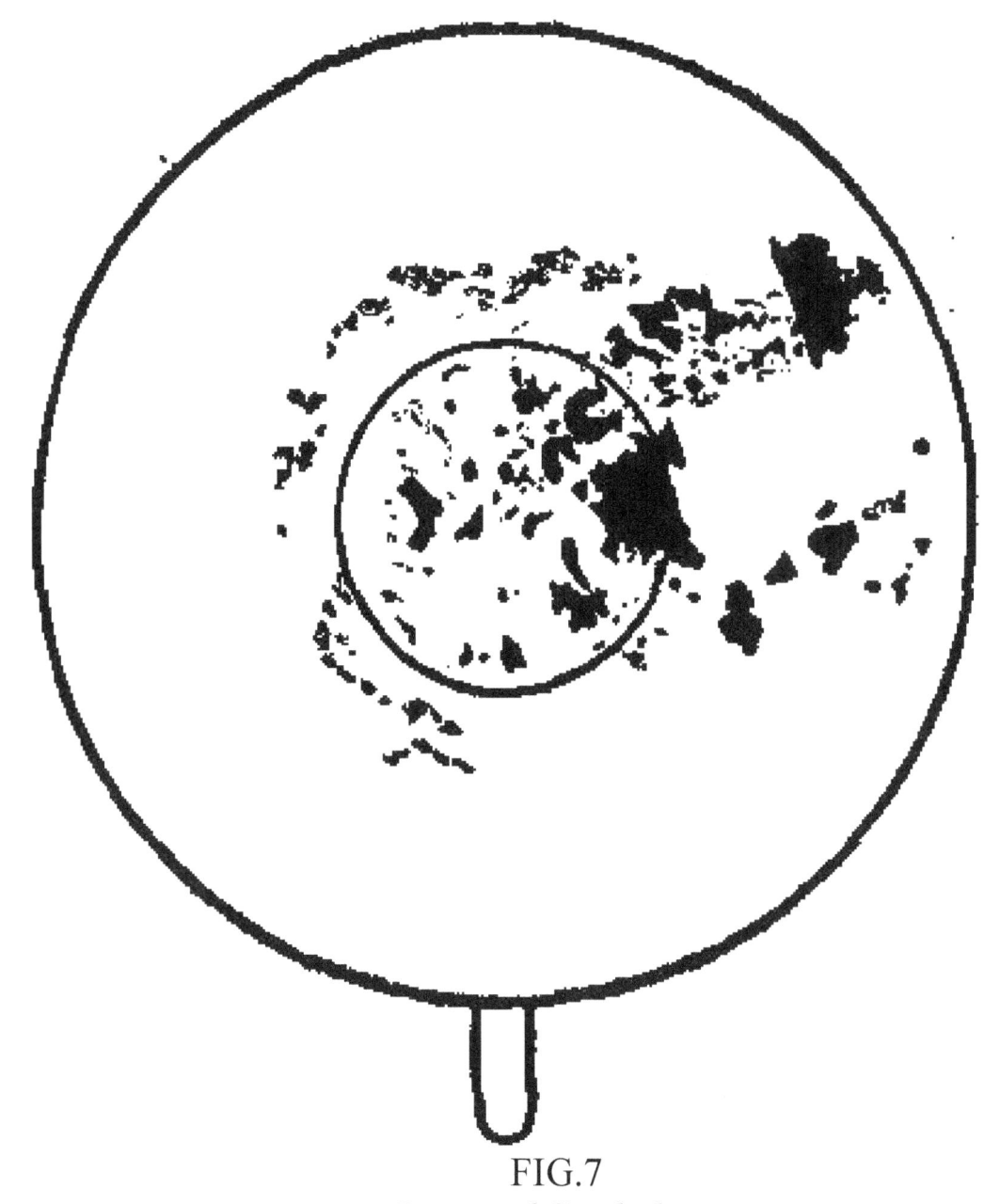

FIG.7

Principal Symbols:—

Large horse-shoe, edge of bottom, in conjunction with smaller horse-shoe.
Line of dots leading E.N.E. to
Large building surmounted by
Tree, overlapping rim.
Flowers.
Small triangles.

Initial 'T' with letter and money signs.

INTERPRETATION
FIG.8

This tea-cup appears to give warning by the flag in conjunction with a rifle and the letter 'V' that some friend of the consultant will be wounded in battle, and as there is a coffin in the bottom of the cup that the wounds will be fatal. On the other side, however, a sceptre, surrounded by signs of honours, seems to indicate that 'V' will be recognized by his sovereign and a decoration bestowed upon him for bravery in battle, shown by the initial 'K' accompanied by a letter-sign, and by the astrological sign of Mars, intervening between these and the sceptre.

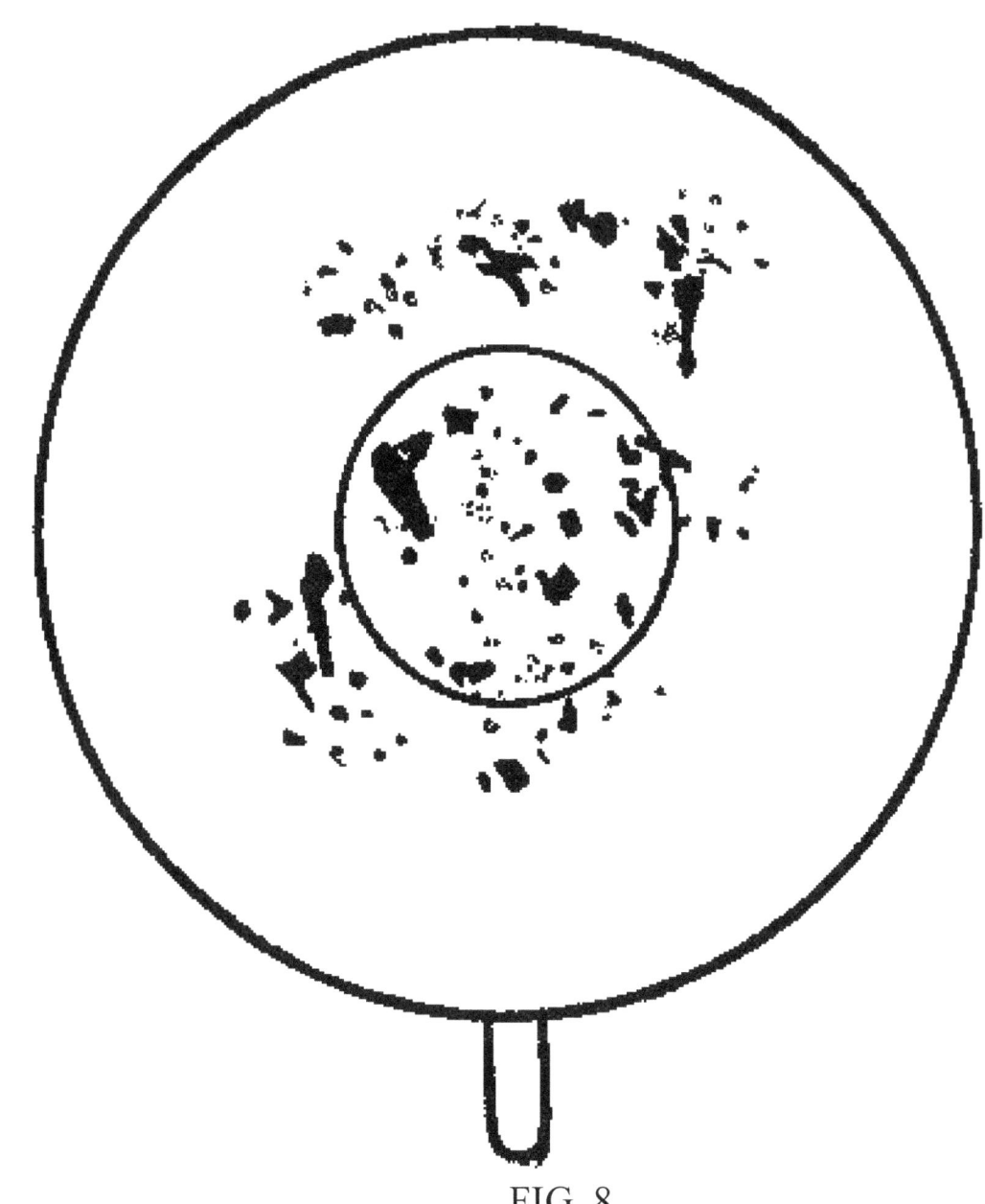

FIG. 8
Principal Symbols:—

Coffin in bottom, in conjunction with 'V.'
Flag in conjunction with rifle on side.
Sceptre on side.
Large initial 'K' with letter sign near sceptre.
Astrological sign of Mars between them.
Initial 'V' near flag and rifle.

INTERPRETATION
FIG. 9

If the consultant be single this cup will, by means of the hare on the side, tell him that he will speedily be married. The figure of a lady holding out an ivy-leaf is a sign that his sweetheart will prove true and constant, and the heart in conjunction with a ring and the initial 'A' still further points to marriage with a person whose name begins with that letter. The flower, triangle, and butterfly are all signs of prosperity, pleasure and happiness.

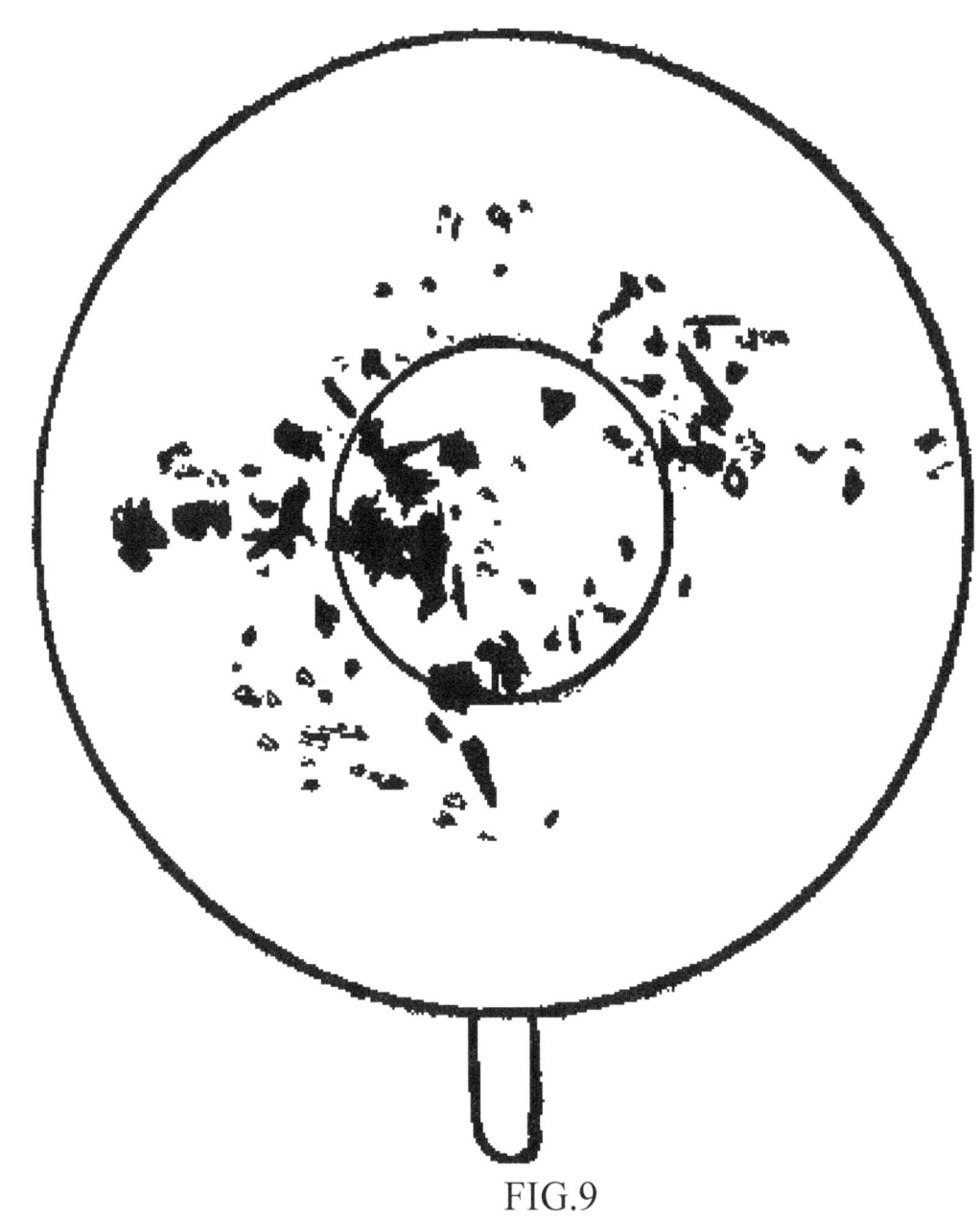

FIG.9

Principal Symbols:—

Hare sitting on side.
Butterfly near rim.
Heart and ring.
Large flower on edge of bottom.
Figure of woman holding ivy-leaf in bottom.
Triangle.
Initials 'A' and small 'C' with dots.

INTERPRETATION
FIG. 10

This is typical of the cup being too often consulted by some people. It is almost void of meaning, the only symbols indicating a short journey, although the flower near the rim denotes good luck, and the fact that the bottom is clear that nothing very important is about to happen to the consultant.

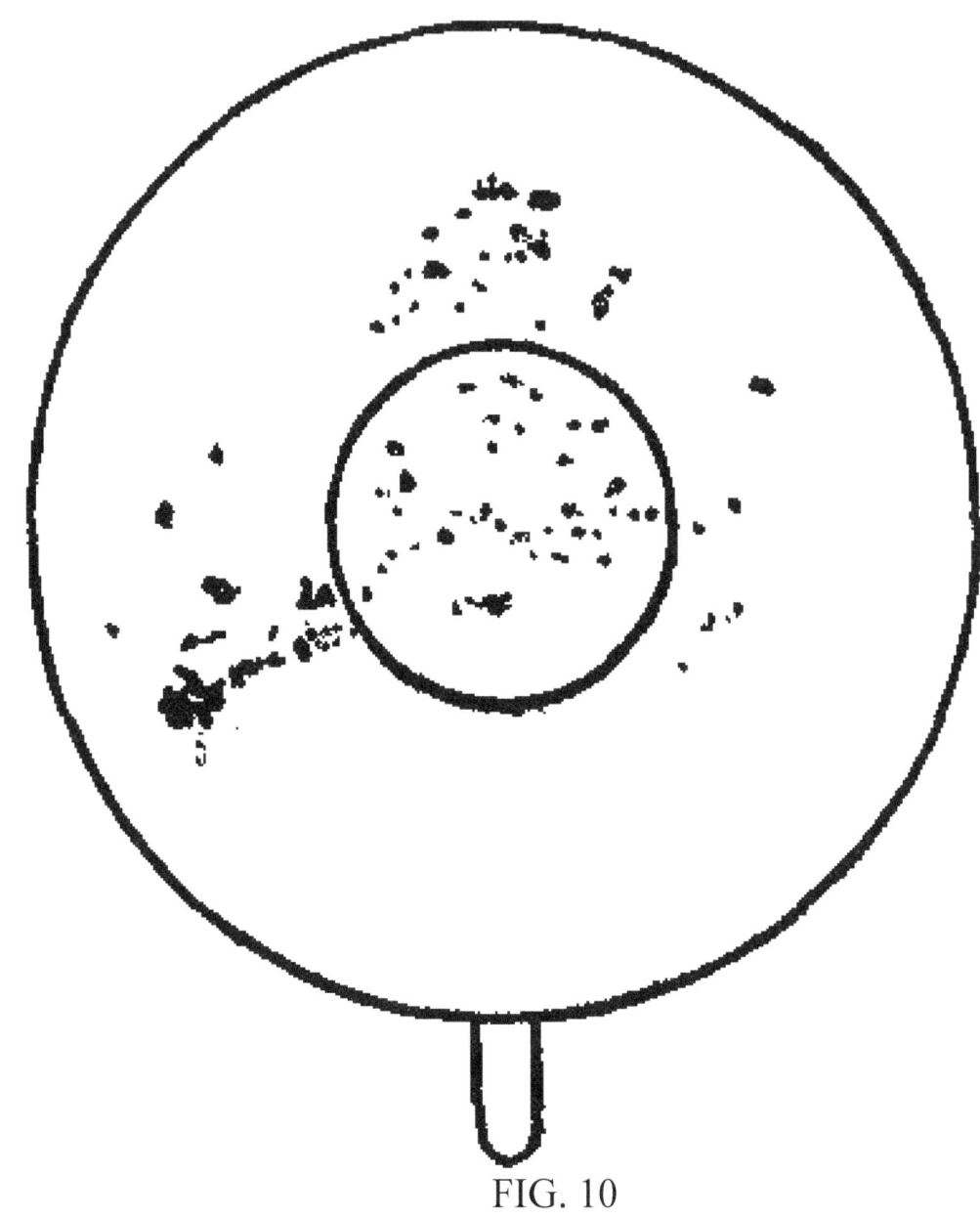

FIG. 10
Principal Symbols:—

Line of dots leading W.S.W to
Flower.
Two letters near rim

CHAPTER VI

OMENS

How have omens been regarded in the past? An appeal to anciency is usually a safeguard for a basis. It is found that most of the earliest records are now subsisting. See official guide to the British Museum. Babylonian and Assyrian antiquities, table case H. Nineveh Gallery, the following appears:

"By means of omen tablets the Babylonian and Assyrian priests from time immemorial predicted events which they believed would happen in the near or in the remote future. They deduced these omens from the appearance and actions of animals, birds, fish, and reptiles; from the appearance of the entrails of sacrificial victims; from the appearance and condition of human and animal offspring at birth; from the state and condition of various members of the human body."

In India, where the records of the early ages of civilization go back hundreds of years, omens are considered of great importance.

Later, in Greece, the home of the greatest and highest culture and civilization, we find, too, omens regarded very seriously, while to-day there are vast numbers of persons of intellect, the world over, who place reliance upon omens.

That there is some good ground for belief in some omens seems indisputable. Whether this has arisen as the result of experience, by the following of some particular event close upon the heels of signs observed, or whether it has been an intuitive science, in which provision has been used to afford an interpretation, is not quite clear. It seems idle to attempt to dismiss the whole thing as mere superstition, wild guessing, or abject credulity, as some try to do, with astrology and alchemy also, and other occult sciences; the fact remains that omens have, in numberless instances, given good warnings.

To say that these are just coincidences is to beg the question. For the universe is governed by law. Things happen because they must, not because they may. There is no such thing as accident or coincidence. We may not be able to see the steps and the connections. But they are there all the same.

In years gone by many signs were deduced from the symptoms of sick men; the events or actions of a man's life; dreams and visions; the appearance of a man's shadow; from fire, flame, light, or smoke; the state and condition of cities and their streets, of fields, marshes, rivers, and lands. From the appearances of the stars and planets, of eclipses, meteors, shooting stars, the direction of winds, the form of clouds, thunder and lightning and other weather incidents, they were able to forecast happenings. A number of tablets are devoted to these prophecies.

It is conceivable that many of these omens should have found their way into Greece, and it is not unreasonable to believe that India may have derived her knowledge of omens from Babylonia; or it may have been the other way about. The greatest of scholars are divided in their opinions as to which really is the earlier civilization.

The point to be made here is that in all parts of the world—in quarters where we may be certain that no trace of Grecian, Indian, or Babylonian science or civilization has appeared—there are to be found systems of prophecies by omens.

It may be accounted for in two ways. One that in all races as they grow up, so to speak, there is the same course of evolution of ideas and superstition which to many appears childish. The other explanation seems to be the more reasonable one, if we believe, as we are forced to do, that omens do foretell—that all peoples, all races, accumulate a record, oral or otherwise, of things which have happened more or less connected with things which seemed to indicate them. In course of time this knowledge appears to consolidate. It gets generally accepted as true. And then it is handed on from generation to generation. Often with the passage of years it gets twisted and a new meaning taken out of it altogether different from the original.

It would be difficult to attempt to classify omens. Many books have been written on the subject and more yet to be written of the beliefs of the various races. The best that can be offered here is a selection from one or other of the varied sources. In Greece sneezing was a good omen and was considered a proof of the truth of what was said at the moment by the sneezer.

A tingling in the hand denoted the near handling of money, a ringing in the ears that news will soon be received. The number of sneezes then became a sign for more definite results. The hand which tingled, either right or left, indicated whether it were to be paid or received. The particular ear affected was held to indicate good or evil news. Other involuntary movements of the body were also considered of prime importance.

Many omens are derived from the observation of various substances dropped into a bowl of water. In Babylon oil was used. To-day in various countries melted lead, wax, or the white of an egg, is used. From the shapes which result, the trade or occupation of a future husband, the luck for the year, and so on, are deduced in the folk practices of modern Europe. Finns use stearine and melted lead, Magyars lead, Russians wax, Danes lead and egg, and the northern counties of England egg, wax and oil.

Bird omens were the subject of very serious study in Greece. It has been thought that this was because in the early mythology of Greece some of their gods and goddesses were believed to have been birds. Birds, therefore, were particularly sacred, and their appearances and movements were of profound significance. The principal birds for signs were the raven, the crow, the heron, wren, dove, woodpecker, and kingfisher, and all the birds of prey, such as the hawk, eagle, or vulture, which the ancients classed together (W. R. Halliday, "Greek Divination"). Many curious instances, which were fulfilled, of bird omens are related in "The Other World," by Rev. F. Lee. A number of families have traditions about the appearance of a white bird in particular.

"In the ancient family of Ferrers, of Chartley Park, in Staffordshire, a herd of wild cattle is preserved. A tradition arose in the time of Henry III. that the birth of a parti-coloured calf is a sure omen of death, within the same year, to a member of the Lord Ferrers family. By a noticeable coincidence, a calf of this description has been born whenever a death has happened of late years in this noble family." (*Staffordshire Chronicle*, July, 1835). The falling of a picture or a statue or bust of the individual is usually regarded as an evil omen. Many cases are cited where this has been soon followed by the death of the person.

It would be easy to multiply instances of this sort: of personal omen or warning. The history and traditions of our great families are saturated with it. The predictions and omens relating to certain well known families, and others, recur at once; and from these it may be inferred that beneath the more popular beliefs there is enough fire and truth to justify the smoke that is produced, and to reward some of the faith that is placed in the modern dreambooks and the books of fate and the interpretations of omens.

OMENS

ACORN.—Falling from the oak tree on anyone, is a sign of good fortune to the person it strikes.

BAT.—To see one in day time means long journey.

BIRTHDAYS.—

"Monday's child is fair of face,
Tuesday's child is full of grace,
Wednesday's child is full of woe,
Thursday's child has far to go,
Friday's child is loving and giving,
Saturday's child works hard for its living;
But a child that's born on the Sabbath-day
Is handsome and wise and loving and gay."

BUTTERFLY.—In your room means great pleasure and success, but you must not catch it, or the luck will change.

CANDLE.—A spark on the wick of a candle means a letter for the one who first sees it. A big glow like a parcel means money coming to you.

CAT.—Black cat to come to your house means difficulties caused by treachery. Drive it away and avoid trouble.

CHAIN.—If your chain breaks while on you means disappointments or a broken engagement of marriage.

CLOTHES.—To put on clothes the wrong way out is a sign of good luck; but you must not alter them, or the luck will change.

CLOVER.—To find a four-leaf clover means luck to you, happiness and prosperity.

COW.—Coming in your yard or garden a very prosperous sign.

CRICKETS.—A lucky omen. It foretells money coming to you. They should not be disturbed.

DOG.—Coming to your house, means faithful friends and a favourable sign.

DEATH-WATCH.—A clicking in the wall by this little insect is regarded as evil, but it does not necessarily mean a death; possibly only some sickness.

EARS.—You are being talked about if your ear tingles. Some say, "right for spite, left for love." Others reverse this omen. If you think of the person, friend, or acquaintance who is likely to be talking of you, and mention the name aloud, the tingling will cease if you say the right one.

FLAG.—If it falls from the staff, while flying it means danger from wounds inflicted by an enemy.

FRUIT STONES OR PIPS.—Think of a wish first, and then count your stones or pips. If the number is even, the omen is good. If odd, the reverse is the case.

GRASSHOPPER in the house means some great friend or distinguished person will visit you.

HORSESHOE.—To find one means it will bring you luck.

KNIVES crossed are a bad omen. If a knife or fork or scissors falls to the ground and sticks in the floor you will have a visitor.

LADYBIRDS betoken visitors.

LOOKING GLASS.—To break means it will bring you ill luck.

MAGPIES.—One, bad luck; two, good luck; three, a wedding; four, a birth.

MARRIAGE.—A maid should not wear colours; a widow

never white. Happy omens for brides are sunshine and a cat sneezing.

MAY.—"Marry in May, and you'll rue the day."

NEW MOON on a Monday signifies good luck and good weather. The new moon seen for the first time over the right shoulder offers the chance for a wish to come true.

NIGHTINGALE.—Lucky for lovers if heard before the cuckoo.

OWLS are evil omens. Continuous hooting of owls in your trees is said to be one of ill-health.

PIGS.—To meet a sow coming towards you is good; but if she turns away, the luck flies.

RABBITS.—A rabbit running across your path is said to be unlucky.

RAT.—A rat running in front of you means treacherous servants and losses through enemies.

RAVEN.—To see one, means death to the aged or trouble generally.

SALT spilled means a quarrel. This may be avoided by throwing a pinch over the left shoulder.

SCISSORS.—If they fall and stick in the floor it means quarrels, illness, separation of lovers.

SERPENT OR SNAKE.—If it crosses your path, means spiteful enemies, bad luck. Kill it and your luck will be reversed.

SHOES.—The right shoe is the best one to put on first.

SHOOTING STARS.—If you wish, while the star is still moving, your wish will come true.

SINGING before breakfast, you'll cry before night.

SPIDERS.—The little red spider is the money spider, and means good fortune coming to you. It must not be disturbed. Long-legged spiders are also forerunners of good fortune.

TOWEL.—To wipe your hands on a towel at the same time with another, means you are to quarrel with him or her in the near future.

WHEEL.—The wheel coming off any vehicle you are riding

in means you are to inherit some fortune, a good omen.

WASHING HANDS.—If you wash your hands in the water just used by another, a quarrel may be expected, unless you first make the sign of the cross over the water.

www.ingramcontent.com/pod-product-compliance
Lightning Source LLC
Chambersburg PA
CBHW081125280526
45787CB00007B/2983